AF661336

For Tia, Bel and Julia, for all their wonderful help with wintry ideas—M.C.

For Zoe, Jade and Ray—D.M.

Scholastic Australia
An imprint of Scholastic Australia Pty Limited
PO Box 579 Gosford NSW 2250
ABN 11 000 614 577
www.scholastic.com.au

Part of the Scholastic Group
Sydney • Auckland • New York • Toronto • London • Mexico City
New Delhi • Hong Kong • Buenos Aires • Puerto Rico

Published by Scholastic Australia in 2023.
Text copyright © Meredith Costain, 2023.
Illustrations copyright © Danielle McDonald, 2023.

The moral rights of Meredith Costain have been asserted.
The moral rights of Danielle McDonald have been asserted.

All rights reserved. No part of this publication may be reproduced or transmitted in any form or by any means, electronic or mechanical, including photocopying, recording, storage in an information retrieval system, or otherwise, without the prior written permission of the publisher, unless specifically permitted under the Australian Copyright Act 1968 as amended.

ISBN: 978-93-5471-613-3

This reprint edition, February 2026

NATIONAL LIBRARY OF AUSTRALIA
A catalogue record for this book is available from the National Library of Australia

Typeset in Sweetie Pie.

Printed in India at Nutech Print Services Pvt. Ltd.

SUPER SPECIAL

Winter Wonders

Monday morning, very, very early

Dear Diary,

I am sitting up in bed totally wide awake, even though it is super, super early. SOOO early even the birds that usually sing joyful songs in the trees outside my bedroom window aren't awake yet.

SOOO early, even the rest of my family aren't awake yet. Not even Dad!

Or Bob!

I am WAY too **SUPER EXCITED** about what's happening today to sleep.

And guess why?

We're going on holiday! To the snow!

And it's going to be our absolutely and totally **BEST HOLIDAY EVER!**

This is because:

a) Zoe (my BFF) is also coming (along with her family), and

(B) I have some brand-new and exceptionally super-stylish outfits to wear, because . . .

(C) we are going to Crystal Mountain. And staying at the fabulous Crystal Mountain Ski Lodge!!!

And also because this will be the very first time I will be seeing (and also walking on and playing in) snow in my WHOLE ENTIRE LIFE!

It's all so EXCITERATING! And SPECIAL!

SOOO special that I am bringing my brand-new giant pack of coloured pencils with me. I can use them to write and draw about all the pazillions of amazing things that are going to happen. And Mum has even lent me her camera so I can take some photos of them as well!

Have to stop writing now, Diary. I can hear rustling and stomping and groaning sounds. Which means everyone else is waking up to get ready for our big trip!

Chat soon!

Yours 4 EVER,

Ella

XOXO

About three hours later, in the car

Dearest Diary,

Everyone took HEAPS of time getting ready to go to the snow this morning.

EsPECially Olivia. ☹

And Max. ☹

And then Nanna Kate—who is going to be looking after Bob while we're away—was late.

And so were Zoe and her mum and her big brother, Will.

So it took about 900 hours (almost) before we were all sitting in the car, ready to go. ☺

Crystal Mountain is exTREMEly far away from where we live. ~~Forch~~ Fortunately, there are pazillions of interesting things to see along the way.

Like pretty birds flitting through towering trees,

and a rushing river under a sweet little bridge,

and a round spikerous creature called an echidna waiting under the towering trees for our cars to go past so it could cross the road.

Dad said I was lucky to see it because echidnas are very shy. I'm going to write all about them later in my *Big Book of Animal Fact Files.*

and UP

and UP

And then we kept driving UP
the windy road until we reached the very
toppest part of the top of the mountain.

And bits of white stuff on the road and
the ground underneath the towering trees
kept getting frostier

and fluffier

and sparklier

until . . . oops!

I have to stop writing for a bit because we just went over a giganterous BUMP!

And another one!

AAARRRGGGHHH!!!

About an hour later . . .

Dear Diary,

We finally arrived at Crystal Mountain Village!

~~(Unforch~~ Unfortunately, Max was a bit carsick during the bumpy part. And threw up all over his car seat. Ewww. ☹)

And guess what was happening?

It was snowing!

Which was amazing! And excellent! And fantabulously fabulous!

And also VERY, VERY COLD!

So we all made sure we zipped up our jackets extra tightly, and put on our woolly hats and scarves and mittens and/or gloves before we climbed out of the car.

Luckily there was a lovely big fireplace inside the ski lodge to warm everyone up again. ☺

I wonder what the other kids staying here are going to be like. I hope they're friendly! ☺

This is a picture of what Zoe and my bedroom looks like. And sadly, also Olivia's. ☹

As you can see, there is a lovely comfy single bed and also a not so lovely uncomfy bunk bed.

Everyone wanted the comfy single bed. So we played a quick game of Rock, Paper, Scissors.

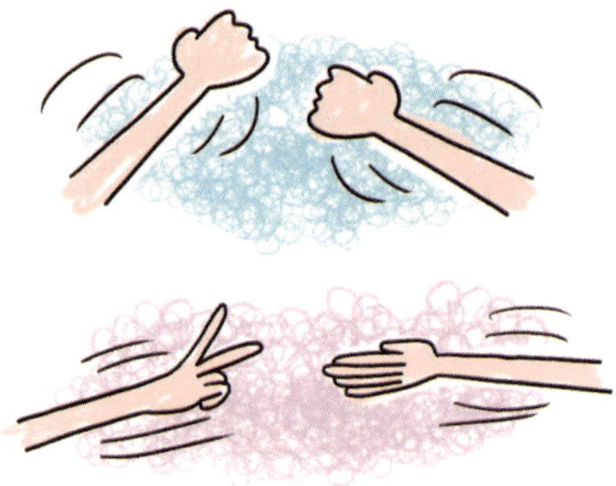

And guess who won?

If you said me then you are **WRONG. WRONG. WRONG!**

It was Olivia. ☹

It's SOOO unfair, Diary. Why does Olivia **always** get the thing I really, really want?

She's probably going to spend the WHOLE TIME we're here sitting up in her special bed like a queen, listening in to EVERY WORD Zoe and I say to each other. ☹☹☹

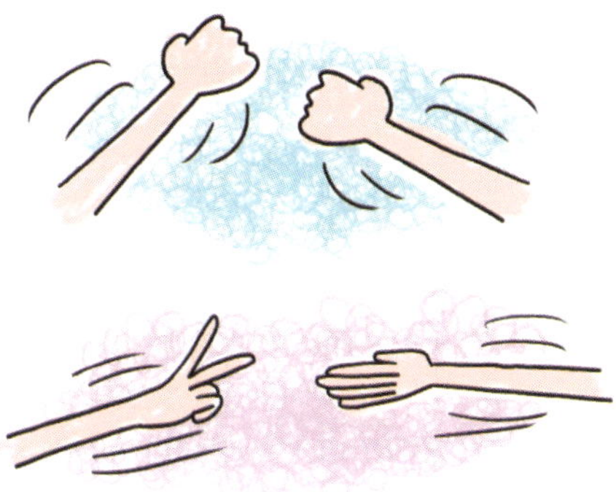

Anyway, after that Zoe and I had another game of Rock, Paper, Scissors to see who got the top bunk.

And this time I won! YES!! Which is just as well, Diary, because NO WAY do I want Olivia to be able to see what I'm writing in you when we're all in bed.

Need to go now, Diary. Dad just knocked on our door to say it's time for dinner!

Chat soon.

Yours truly,
Ella
XOXO

Monday night, in bed, very, VERY late

Guess what I just heard?

A super scary howling sound!

Like this:

AAARRRROOO-OWWWRRR!

And it was coming from OUTSIDE MY WINDOW!

I hope it doesn't come inside!

E

Tuesday, after breakfast

Dear Diary,

Zoe and I woke up as soon as the sun peeked through our curtains this morning. And guess what we saw when we looked out the window?

If you said the thing I heard howling last night, you are wrong.

It was . . .

MORE SNOW!

Pazillions of it, all piled up outside our ski lodge.

So we climbed into our toasty warm snow gear, and raced outside to play. Dad and Max, and Zoe's big brother, Will, came too. ☺

We rolled the snow up into little balls and threw them at each other.

Then we built a big messy snowman. We even tied a woolly scarf around his neck so he wouldn't get cold. ☺☺☺

And guess what?

A boy and a girl, who looked almost exACTly the same as each other, came over to play in the snow with us. They lay down on their backs, then waved their arms and legs up and down and from side to side, making pretty patterns in the snow. Like this.

Zoe and I were BUSTING to know what they were doing. So we asked them.

So we did!

Some other kids from our ski lodge came running out and had snowball fights and/or made snow angels too.

It was funnerous fun!

And then after that we all tromped back inside and had a giganterous breakfast with our new friends. Doing snow stuff makes you SUPER hungry. ☺

I'll be back soon. Mum's taking us to a **big snow gear hiring place** so we can get all the things we need for FUN IN THE ~~SUN~~ SNOW!

CU Later,

Snowygator! ☺

Ella

XOXO

Tuesday, before dinner

Dear Diary,

We went to the snow gear hire place!

On the way, we saw some kids snowboarding. Some of them were even doing sweet little jumpy things over bumps in the snow. It looked aMAZing! I hope we get to do that while we're here.

And guess who was at the snow hire place when we got there?

The **Snow Angel twins!** We even found out their names.

The snow hire place belongs to Lizzy and Leo's uncle and aunty. And Lizzy and Leo were there because they were helping people who know NOTHING about being at the snow* to find everything they needed.

* Like us!

First of all they asked us some **importerant questions** about our plans for the week.

And then they took us on a tour of the shop so we could check out **all the stuff** we needed. (Except for the hot tub. ~~Forch~~ Fortunately there's already one of those in our ski lodge. ☺)

Here are some of the things we hired:

WaterPROOF **Jackets**

WaterPROOF **OVERALLS**

They also had lots of sweet little beanies and scarves to keep your head and neck warm, that you could buy.

But we didn't. We've already got HEAPS of these.

And then I saw THIS one!

It would be PERFECT for Max to wear when he's making his giganterous snow monsters. So I BEGGED Mum to buy it for him.

And guess what she said?

HINT: Her answer **doesn't** rhyme with snow.

So we bought the furry bear hat for Max! And now he wears it EVERYWHERE!

Zoe and I spent AGES picking out our snowboards. There were so many different designs!

This is the one I ended up choosing.

That's because the dolphins on it look **EXACTLY** like the ones I saw when I went on a beach holiday with Zoe.

(And also, because **mauve** is my most FAVOURITEST colour. ☺) So I think it could be a really, REALLY lucky snowboard!

Lizzy and Leo told us we had both made excellent choices! And that we should sign up straightaway for snowboarding lessons with their Uncle Lenny.

YES! We both thought that was a wonderful idea. We just needed to ask our mums first.

So we're going! The lessons start tomorrow at 9.00 am.

And Zoe's big brother is coming along as well!

I can't wait!

Yours 4 Ever,
Ella

Tuesday night, in bed

Dear Diary,

I have so much more to tell you about what happened today!

There are six other kids staying at our ski lodge, including Maisie and Jana, who are now Olivia's bestest new BFFs*. They all went tobogganing together after lunch.

* which is a BIG RELIEF for Zoe and me, Diary. Because it means Olivia won't want to follow us around ALL DAY snooping on our every move like she usually does.

And Max has a new friend too, called Hari. They made giganterous snow monsters outside our lodge today.

Hari's dad showed them how to poke two holes in their snow monsters' faces to make their eyes. And then they pushed glow sticks inside the holes.

This is what happened when it started to get dark tonight! ☺

SPOOOOOKY! ☺

SOOO spooky I used Mum's special camera to get a photo of them in case no-one believes me!

Max is totally (and also completely and utterly) OBSESSED* with monsters—especially SNOW monsters—right now.

* Obsessed means when you are constantly thinking about something (for example, a freshly baked yummerous jam doughnut) ALL THE TIME and you CANNOT STOP, not even if a herd of hungry hyenas was following you!

SOOO obsessed, he wants me to read him **ALL the parts** about snow monsters in his favourite book**, whenever it's my turn to read him his bedtime story.

** which is called *My Big Book of Monsters*.

Like tonight.

So I read him the part all about Yetis.

Yetis are these really weird creatures that some people say they've seen hanging around the snowy slopes of the Himalayan mountains. They're also known as Abominable Snowmen. (Sometimes.) And guess what? Some people say there's another creature just like them in North America. Called Bigfoot! ☺

And this is what Yetis are supposed to look like.

And they make a horrendously horrible howling sound when they're prowling around at night.

Like this:

AAARRROOO-OWWWRRR!

And guess what else?

Some stories say that their feet ~~acksh~~ actually face back to front! Like this:

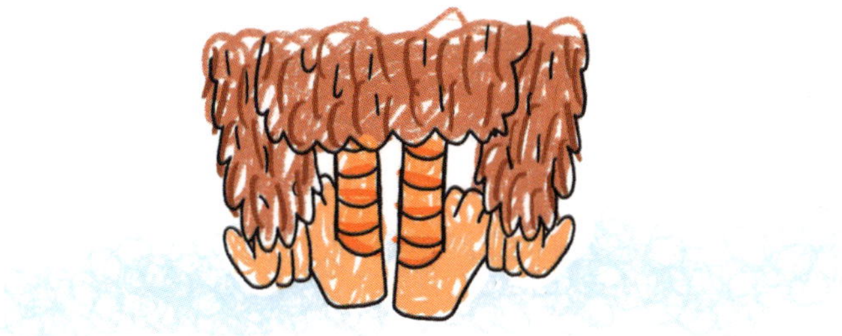

So the best way to get away from a Yeti if it is chasing after you is to run exTREMEly fast down a steeperous hill!

I hope there **aren't** any Yetis (or Abominable Snowmen and/or Bigfoots) on Crystal Mountain!

Good night
Sleep tight
Don't let
the Yetis
BITE!

Love,
Ella

Tuesday night, in bed, super, super late

Guess what I just heard?

The same super-scary howling sound I heard last night!

And it was coming from OUTSIDE MY WINDOW again!

I hope it isn't one of Max and Hari's snow monsters!

E 😮

About two minutes later . . .

Or maybe it's a . . . a . . . Yeti! 😮😮

About two minutes after that . . .

Or a Bigfoot!

Or an Abominable Snowman! 😮😮😮

About 11.45 seconds after that . . .

I was so scared that there was a Yeti (or an Abominable Snowman or Bigfoot) lurking around in the snow outside our ski lodge that I quickly woke up Zoe (and also Olivia) to see if they'd heard the howling sound as well.

And guess what?

They hadn't.

Wednesday, before dinner

Dearest Diary,

Getting ready for a big day on the slopes is VERY HARD WORK!

First of all Zoe and I did some complicated leg stretching,

and also squatterous squatting, so our legs wouldn't turn into soggy bits of jelly while we were having our snowboarding lesson. Which would be SUPER embarrassing.

And then we had a giganterous breakfast* to make sure we had MOUNTAINS of ENERGY to keep us going ALL DAY LONG!

* Waffles! (Yum!) With bananas and maple syrup! And hot chocolate with frotherous frothy bits!

As soon as breakfast was over Zoe and I put on our warmest underclothing

and our waterproof ski jackets and overalls

and our woolly scarves and snow gloves and snow boots and helmets and goggles.

And then we stumbled out the front door of our ski lodge and headed off to the snowfields with Will. Wobbling about like big **HUNKY CHUNKY FUNKY** pumpkins! ☺

Leo and Lizzy and their Uncle Lenny and some other kids were already there when we arrived at the snowboarding lesson place.

It was on a sweet little gentle sloping hill on the other side of the big chairlift.

Lizzy said it's called a bunny slope. Which is REALLY WEIRD to the power of a pazillion and six, Diary, because I didn't see any bunnies anywhere. Not even teensy tiny ones.

My lucky dolphin snowboard was getting a bit heavy. So I put it down on the ~~ground~~ snow to let my arm have a nice rest.

And then all of a suddenly . . .

The Bad News

. . . it went whooshing away down the bunny slope.

The Badder News

I tried to run after it, but my hunky chunky pumpkin outfit made me too slow.

The ~~Worserer~~ Even Worse News

I tripped over a big mound of snow. ☹

The Horrendously Horrible News

All the other kids in the White Wombats snowboarding group (except for Zoe) started laughing at me. Which was really unfair, Diary, because it wasn't even my fault.

The Good News

Zoe's big brother kindly tromped down the slope and helped me to stand up again. And also—very slowly—helped me get back up to the top part again.

The ~~Gooder~~ Even Better News

And Lizzy and Leo whizzed even further down the slope and rescued my snowboard. Then carried it all the way back up again, where we had a BIG TEARY REUNION. (Me and my lucky snowboard, I mean. ☺)

And then everyone* said they were very sorry for laughing at me.

* Except for this boy called Flick who was wearing a ski jacket with crocodiles all over it.

He just stared at me with a **sharkerous smile** instead. Which was just WEIRD, with a capital W.

And then we all** stopped being teary and saying sorry and Leo and Lizzy's Uncle Lenny started the snowboarding lesson.

** Except for Flick.

First of all, he moved us all across to a nicer, **FLATTER part** of the bunny slope so we wouldn't all go whooshing off like my snowboard did.

Then he told us to NEVER put your snowboard down on the snow with the flat side facing down if you are standing on a slope. And to put it **UPSIDE DOWN** instead, so that the foot binding parts are resting on the snow.

After that, Uncle Lenny showed us how to **buckle our feet** into the foot binding parts. But first we had to work out which of our feet was the main, strongest one, to go on the **back part** of the board.

Zoe and I weren't sure if our left foot was the strongest one, or the right.

So we asked Uncle Lenny how we could tell.

And guess what he said?

And then he asked Zoe which foot she stuck out to help get her balance back if she slipped on something.

Then Uncle Lenny told us there are special names for the way you put your feet on your snowboard. And they're called GOOFY and REGULAR.

And guess which one I am?

GOOFY ☺☺☺

And guess what else? Only two of us out of the whole group have goofy feet. Me and a boy called Cody. It made me feel really special. ☺

Next Uncle Lenny showed us some different ways to move across the snow.

Like SKATING,
where you push
yourself along with
your back foot,

This one
was
HEAPS
FASTER
than Skating

and
GLIDING
with only the
front foot
buckled into
the binding
part,

and doing little bunny hops into the air, with BOTH feet buckled in.

THIS ONE was THE MOST FUN

And then we all started SLOWLY and GENTLY twisting and turning down the slope on our snowboards.

I was going really, really, REALLY well until . . .

"Da da Da... DUMMM."

Someone called out my name. Really, really loudly.

So loudly, I turned around to see who it was.

And lost my balance.

And . . .

SPLATTTT!

. . . did a giganterous **FACEPLANT** into the snowy snow. ☹☹☹

And guess who it was calling out?

HINT: Her name rhymes with this place.

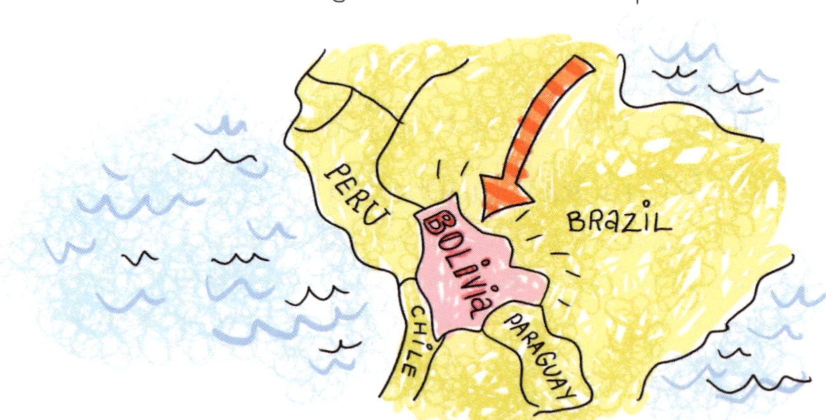

If you said Olivia you are 100 per cent

And guess what? That Flick boy with the weird ski jacket laughed at me AGAIN. Really loudly this time.

No-one else laughed though. They just (kindly) helped me up instead.

Lizzy and Leo did **a big glare** at Flick.

Then they told me I'd been snowboarding really, really well until my ~~unforch~~ unfortunate (and also unforeseen) accident. Which made me feel really, really happy again! ☺☺

After that, Zoe and I did a bit more snowboarding practice with Will (who is a bazillion times better than everyone else*) and Cody and Layla. And this time I didn't fall over. Not even once! ☺

* Probably because he is already an EXcellent skateboarder. And Uncle Lenny told us lots of the moves are the same.

I've got PAZILLIONS more to tell you about today, Dearest Diary, but it will have to wait until later.

That's because it's dinner time! YUM!

And then Cody and Layla and some of the other White Wombats are coming to our lodge to watch a movie with us. YES!

Talk soon.

Love,

Ella x

Wednesday night, after dinner

Dear Diary-doo,

The man showing the movie is having trouble getting his projectoring thing working. So I sneaked back to my room to write a bit more about the INCREDIBLY EXCITERATING (and also SPINE-TINGLINGLY THRILLING!) things that happened today before it starts.

I hope Olivia doesn't come in and RUIN EVERYTHING like she usually does. ☹

So anyway, after snowboarding, we had lunch and then went on a nature walk with Lumi*, the local ranger.

* Lumi comes from Finland. And guess what her name means?

HINT: It rhymes with this.

If you said 'snow' you are 100 per cent correct! Which means that Lumi has the **PERFECT name** for her job here at Crystal Mountain. ☺

But first we needed to go back to the snow gear hiring place with Dad to get the right stuff for **nature walks** in the snow.

Leo and Lizzy helped us to find exactly what we needed.

Here's what we all said.

Leo (helpfully): You'll need some of these snowshoes.

Lizzy (also helpfully): And also some of these poles. Where are you going?

Me (excitedly): On a nature walk. With Lumi, the ranger.

Lizzy: Why?

Zoe (also excitedly): Because we both ♥ animals. Especially horses.

Me (excitedlier): And also dogs. And dolphins. And we want to see what kinds of animals live in the snow.

(I ~~acksh~~ actually had another VERY SPECIAL importerant reason for wanting to go on the nature walk, but I didn't want them to think I was being **a silly billy**. So I didn't tell ANYONE what it was.)

Lizzy (eagerly): Leo and I ♥ animals too.
Leo: Animals are the BEST. Especially the ones up here. Hey, do you mind if we come with you?
Zoe and me (together): That would be aMAZing!

So then Lizzy and Leo begged their Uncle Lenny to let them come with us on the nature walk as well. And he said yes!

As long as they came back to help him pack everything up at the end of the day.

So we ALL went. ☺

Lizzy and Leo helped us to put on our snowshoes. Then we all hiked off through the trees with Lumi and some other kids also staying on the mountain.

walking with snowshoes on is **completely different** from walking without snowshoes. And also VERY HARD WORK! But our legs got used to it after a while. (Mostly.)

Hopefully Mum will let me join her later in the **hot tub!**

Here are some of the animals we saw on our **nature walk**:

- a mama wombat with her baby

- a brush-tailed rock-wallaby

- a gang-gang cockatoo in the trees

a mountain pygmy possum

Which was SUPER SUPER tiny.

SOOO TINY we almost MISSED it!

a long-nosed potoroo.

I can't wait to write some Animal Fact Files about them! ☺

We saw lots of different **animal tracks** too.

Like these ones.

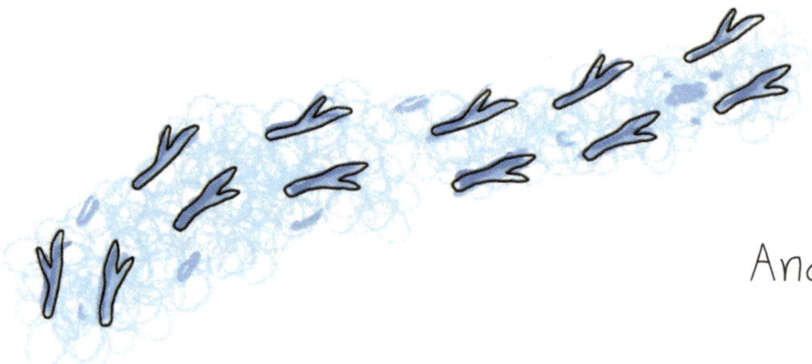

And these ones.

And these ones!

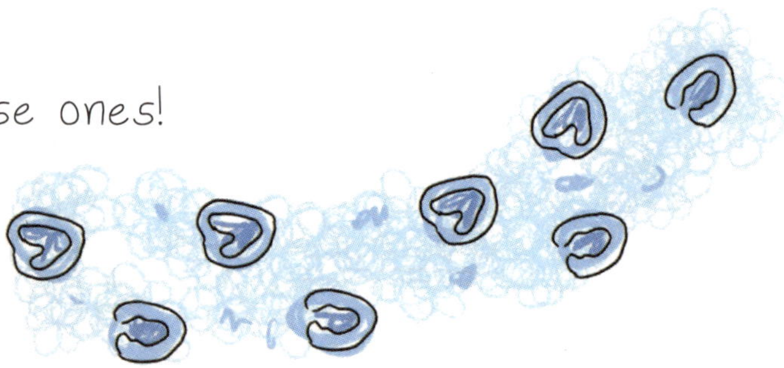

Zoe looked at me with **SHINY EYES**. As shiny as the sun glinting off the icicles hanging from the front window of our ski lodge.

And then she looked at Lumi.

And then Lumi told us all about the wild horses that live in the mountains. They're called brumbies. And they look like this.

Zoe and I spent the rest of our nature walk looking around hopefully for more tracks.

Just in case there were any **beautiful brumbies** prancing around nearby, flicking their bushy manes and tails.

But sadly, we didn't see any. ☹

However, we did see THESE!

They were **HUGE!** And also kind of . . . WEIRD. Like they'd been made by something with giganterous feet, just like a . . .

No. It couldn't be.

Not a yeti. Yetis live in the Himalayan mountains, far far away.

Or could it? They were HEAPS bigger than any of the tracks we'd seen so far.

Or maybe they'd been made by a Bigfoot.

Or . . . **Da da Da . . . DUMMM.**

AN ABOMINABLE SNOWMAN!!!

And that's what's been making the howling noises I've been hearing every night!!

I didn't want to tell anyone about it though, in case they all thought I was just being a big silly billy.

Not even Zoe.

(And esPECially not Olivia.)

Yours truly,
Ella

Wednesday night, in bed

Dear Diary,

Once the projector was fixed we finally watched the movie! It was called Ski Rescue, and it was all about two kids who were sensational at skiing (and also rescuing things).

And it was amazing. And excellent. And fantabulously fabulous!

Maybe one day, if I get even betterer at snowboarding, a famous international movie directorer might make a movie about ME! ☺

Anyway, there was this really interesting part in the movie where Morgan and Raven (the two main stars) follow some tracks in the show. That's because they're looking for a lady and a baby kitten they need to rescue.

And it gave me a really brilliant (and also excellent) idea.

While we were having snacks and hot chocolate by the fireplace after the movie, I could ask the other kids if they'd ever seen any weird-looking tracks in the snow*.

* Like the ones I'd seen this morning when we were out on our nature walk with Lumi.

So I did!

(Which was very, VERY brave—and also courageous and fearless—of me.)

Unfortunately, Flick had come to see the movie too. Cody or Layla must have told him about it. And he was being **really annoying** again.

Like talking over the top of everyone. Or chewing really loudly. And hogging the **comfiest beanbags** so Zoe and I had to sit on lumpy old cushions. ☹

Flick knows HEAPS about weird tracks in the snow though.

Here's what we all said.

Me (nervously): Ummm . . . you know in the movie when Morgan and Raven follow the tracks to rescue the baby kitten?

Layla: Sure. They were SOOOO brave.

Me: Well, this morning Zoe and I saw some REALLY WEIRD tracks.

Zoe: TOTALLY weird.

Me: And I was . . . ummm . . . wondering what might have made them.

Cody: What did they look like?

Me: Kind of like human feet, only HEAPS bigger.

Zoe: Heaps.

Flick (knowledgeably): It was probably just the Yowser.

Layla: What's a Yowser?

Flick: A Yowser is this scary creature that's really, really tall.

Arnie: And it's got super-enormous feet.

Chloe: With six toes on each foot!

Flick: No it doesn't. It's got big googly red eyes though.

Chloe: And they glow in the dark!

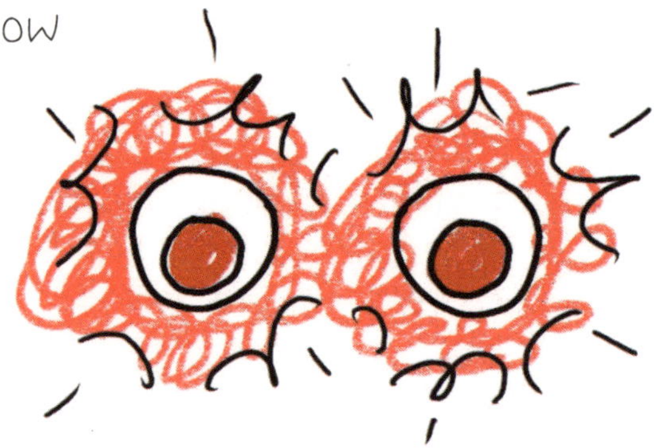

Riley: And its eyes are on the back of its head, instead of on the front.

Flick: No they're not. They're where eyes always are.

Big googly eyes? That glow in the dark? That sounded **exACTly** like what I saw out my window!

Maybe it's not a Yeti or a Bigfoot or an **Abominable Snowman** out there in the dark doing all that horrible howling. Maybe it's actually a **Yowser!**

I asked some more questions to be 100 per cent sure.

Me: Do Yowsers make any sounds?
Flick: Yep.
Me: Like what?
Chloe: Like this. Yip yipppety yip yip YOWWWWWWser.
Flick: No they don't. They go like this.

AAARRRROOO-OWWWRRR!

Wow! The howl Flick howled was (kind of) exACTly the same howl I've been hearing from my top bunk every night.

And it sounds like the tracks I saw in the snow—and also the glowing red googly eyes I saw out the window—are (almost) exACTly the same as the ones Flick and the other kids just described.

Which means the **scary animal** waking me up every night isn't a Yeti.

It's a . . .

wait for it . . .

YOWSER!

Wowsers!

Ella xoxo

PS I hope it doesn't have any friends!

Wednesday, in the middlest part of the middle of the night

Thursday, before lunch

Dear Diary,

The sky was sunny and blue and there was a happy, friendly gentle breeze blowing when Zoe and I set off for our snowboarding lesson this morning.

And guess what we saw on the way?

A sled. With people inside it. Being pulled along by the MOST BEAUTIFUL and CUDDLIEST DOGS I have ever seen in the WHOLE WILD WORLD!

So beautiful I took some photos of them so I can keep them forever and ever. ☺

They're called huskies. And they have thick **woolly coats** that makes them the perfect dog if you are living in a snowy place like Crystal Mountain. Or Siberia, which is where they come from.

They also have **pointy markings** on their face that make them look a bit like Dracula. ☺

And **sticky-up ears** shaped like triangles. And they don't bark like Bob and other dogs do. They howl instead.

Like this. AAAAA-RRRROOOOOOOOOO!

But the **most special thing** about huskies is that their eyes are sometimes different colours. They might have one blue and one brown!

I was just asking the sled tour man if I could pat some of his huskies after the sled came back when I heard a little squeal.

And **guess where** it was coming from?

Zoe!

That's because she'd discovered these **sweet little pups** sitting up in an old sled, waiting for their mama to come back from the sled tour.

And the sled tour man let us hold them and give them a cuddle.

Dogs are my number one, most favouritest animals. So it was the best, most aMAZing thing to ever happen to me! ☺☺☺

SOOO amazing, I wrote this sweet little poem about them. ☺

Husky PUPPIES
FLOPPY, fluffy
Cute and SCRUFFY
wriggling, wiggling, jiggling
Cuddling into MY arms
ADORABLE!

I wish we could get some husky puppies. If we had some at home I would spend my WHOLE ENTIRE DAY (and also some of the night) looking after and/or playing with and cuddling them.

I'm not 100 per cent sure Mum and Dad will let me get some though. So I made this table with my top reasons For and Against to help me convince them.

Reasons FOR	Reasons AGAINST
They are very cute. 	There isn't any snow where we live.
They are very adorable.	They probably need HEAPS of exercise ALL the time.
They are very cuddly.	They probably eat a LOT of food. 
	Bob probably wouldn't be very happy about having new (cuter and more adorable than him) puppies living here.

Sadly, there ended up being more reasons on the AGAINST side of my table than on the FOR side. So I don't think my plan to convince Mum and Dad to let me get our own husky puppies is going to work. ☹

I was just about to screw my table up and throw it in the bin when I had another one of my BRILLIANT THOUGHTS.

Maybe I can just come back to Crystal Mountain every year and visit them instead. YES! That is an Excellent idea.

Now all I have to do is convince Mum and Dad (and the rest of our family) to come with me. ☺

Be back soon, Diary. Olivia and her friends just **banged on the door** to let us know Mum says Zoe and I have to come to the dining room for lunch. Right now straightaway IMMEDIATELY.

Chat soon!

E xOx

About 36.37 minutes later

I'm back! We had veal schnitzels for lunch. And everyone said they were YUM! I'm going to ask Dad if he can make them at home for us.

We all* learnt how to do ollies today!

*Except for Will, as it's also a skateboard move. So he was already SUPER good at it!

And then Uncle Lenny told us something really exciting. SO exciting, I can hardly wait until the weekend for it to happen.

There's going to be a big skiing and snowboarding competition on Saturday morning! With separate groupings for all the different levels.

Like Beginners.

And Middlers.

And Super Expert
Hotshot Whizzes.

And Uncle Lenny told us he thinks we're the best Beginners class he's ever had.

And that Zoe and I (and also Flick and Layla and Cody) should DEFINITELY enter. And that we all have a **really good chance of winning!** We just need to do HEAPS of practice on the **bunny slope** first.

It's all so **THRILLING!** And also **EXCITERATING!!!** ☺

Flick swanned around like a **big swannerous swan**, making sure everyone knew what Uncle Lenny had said.

Which is SO not true, Diary. Cody and Will are HEAPS betterer at snowboarding than Flick. EsPECially Will.

But then Uncle Lenny said Will is SO GOOD he should enter the Middlers section instead, to give all the other Beginners a chance! ☺

Zoe and I looked at each other with SHINY EYES. So shiny we could see Uncle Lenny's glittery snowboarding helmet reflected in them.

Winning the Beginners Snowboarding Competition would be amazing. And excellent. And fantabulously FABulous!

I still need to do pazillions of practices though. Especially on the tricky turning parts as you go down the hill, which can sometimes get a bit WOBBLY.

And also lots of leg-strengthening exercises.

Just as well I have my lucky leaping dolphin snowboard to help me ZOOM across the snow! ☺☺☺

Zoe and I were just setting off down the bunny slope* to practise our turns when something **horrendously horrible** happened.

* Making sure we kept an eye out for any stray bunnies that might accidentally ~~run~~ hop in front of us.

So horrendously horrible (and also tragical) I'm going to have to **stop writing** for a moment so I can wipe away a trickling tear.

The sunny blue sky stopped being sunny and blue, and became covered in **clouderous clouds** instead.

And the gentle breeze turned into a **howling hurricane**. Almost as loud as the howling I heard outside my window again last night.

So we all stopped snowboarding down the bunny slope and headed back to our ski lodges and/or hotels instead. And now we're going to be stuck inside being **bored** to the power of a pazillion and six* for the WHOLE REST OF THE DAY.

☹☹☹

* Or annoyed by annoying little sisters.

It is so not fair, Diary. How am I going to win the Beginners section of the snowboarding competition if I can't practise? It would be like trying to remember all your lines for the school play without getting the chance to rehearse for it.

Yours in desperating despair,

Ella

XX

Thursday, after dinner

Dearest Diary,

Being stuck inside for the whole of the rest of the day wasn't boring at all. In fact it was **funnerous fun!**

That's because we did heaps of **different crafty things**, like making snowflakes out of ice-cream sticks, or cardboard and salt. We even made snow ice-cream!

YUM!!!!

Carly and her mum, Lottie, showed us how to make them. Carly and Lottie stay here at Crystal Mountain Ski Lodge every year.

And Lottie teaches art in a school, just like our excellent (and exceptionally stylish) art teacher, Ms Kahlo. Lottie is quite stylish as well. I bet they'd be REALLY good BFFs if they ever met. ☺

We raided all the cupboards in the Activity Centre, looking for stuff we needed for our craft projects.

Here's what we used to make the silver glitter snowflakes.

First of all we painted the wooden sticks in different colours. I chose mauve for mine. ☺

Then we glued the sticks on top of each other at different angles, to make them look like snowflakes.

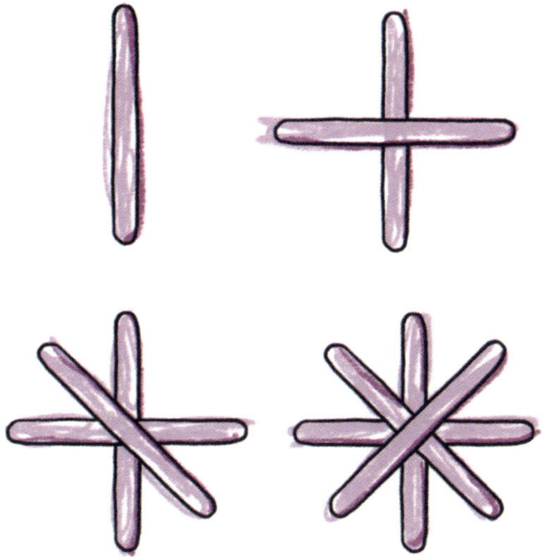

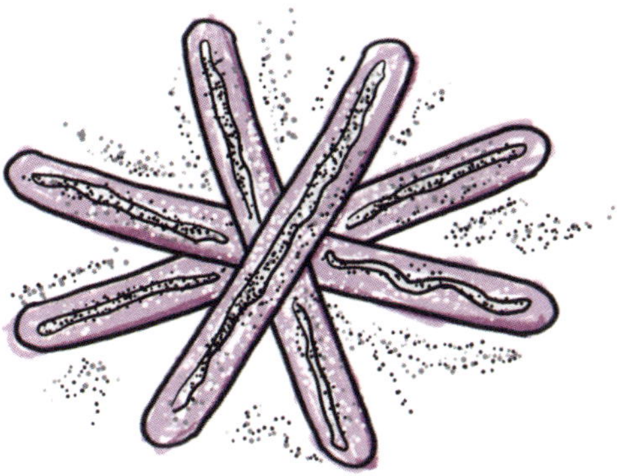

We dabbed glue on top of some of the sticks with a paintbrush. Then we sprinkled lots of silvery glitter on top of the glue.

And we stuck strips of silver glitter stickers to the rest.

Olivia knocked a whole container of sticky red paint over while she was painting her wooden sticks. (Probably because she was talking too much to her friends instead of watching what she was doing.)

And it went EVERYWHERE! (Eww.)

So everyone had to stop painting and gluing and glittering while Zoe and I helped Lottie to clean it all up. ☹

We needed paint for the next activity too. But this time we made sure to keep Olivia **WELL AWAY** from any of the paint containers. Even the ones that weren't open. ☺

We started off by drawing snowflake shapes onto bits of thick cardboard. (I used some of my special new pencils to do this. ☺)

Then we squeezed glue out of our glue bottles onto the lines that we'd drawn.

And then we sprinkled salt all over the gluey bits. Which was really, really, REALLY hard to do without getting it all over the cardboard—and also the table (and us!)—as well.

So Lottie told us to pick up our pieces of cardboard and to

SHAKE SHAKE SHAKE

all the extra bits of salt off.

So we did! And it was funnerous fun!

It was like it was snowing INside the Activity Room, as well as OUTside it. ☺

Then we all grabbed our paintbrushes and dipped them into our watercolour paint. And then **gently brushed them** onto the salty parts with teeny tiny tapperous little taps.

And then . . .

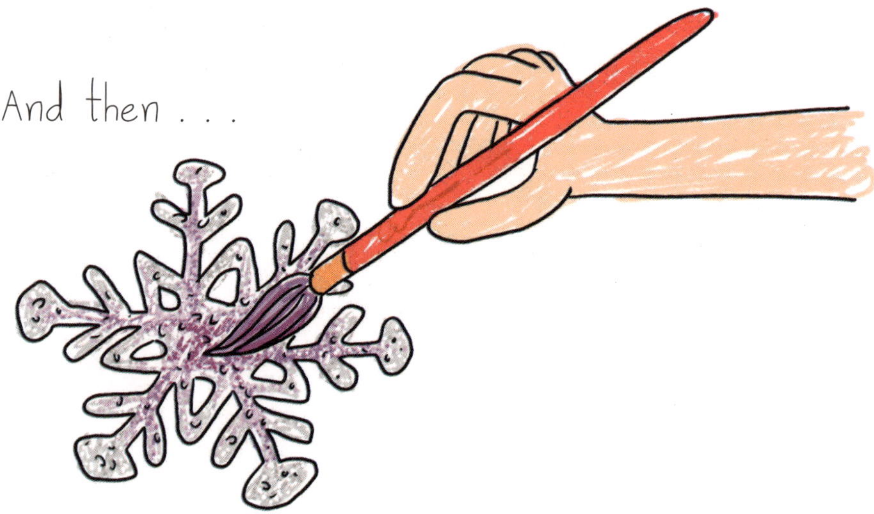

WHOOOOSHHHH!

. . . the salt MAGICALLY soaked up all the colour from our brushes!

We kept on painting with different coloured paints until our snowflakes looked like this.

Have to go now. Zoe and I and our new friends are going back to the Activity Centre to play some board games. Wish me luck!

Yours truly,
Ella

Friday morning, after breakfast

Dear Diary,

Max is SUPER upset. He wanted to wear his lovely bear hat to breakfast but he couldn't find it ANYwhere.

And neither could Mum. Or Dad. Even though they spent (almost) FOREVER looking for it.*

* Which means Dad is now also super upset, because everyone else had eaten all his favourite goodies from the breakfast buffet by the time he got there.

But guess what?

Lottie and Carly went out for a quick ski early this morning. And look what they found under a tree?

Max's hat! But now it's all wet and dirty and sad looking. So he doesn't want to wear it anymore. ☹

I wonder how it got there?

Hmmm.

OOOOOOO! I know! It probably got taken by the Yowser! I heard it howling horrendously again last night. But this time, it sounded even closer to my room.

I wonder if it left any fingerprints on the hat with its **horrible hairy fingers?**

Got to go now, Diary. Zoe's calling me to hurry up and get moving!

E

Friday lunchtime

Dearest Diary,

Zoe and I are sitting in the **Crystal Cafe**, waiting for the rest of our families to turn up so we can all have a lovely special lunch together.

However, they are all **exTREMEly late**. SOOO late we are both **exTREMEly bored**. So Zoe is reading a magazine all about brumbies. And I am pretending* to be doing a special project on Cafes of the World.

* In case anyone asks what I'm writing about.

We left our snowboards on a big rack outside the cafe. (Which is obviously there so people don't tromp snow all over their lovely floor and/or crash into other ~~cusstimers~~ customers.) I hope we can find them again OK!

So anyway, Zoe and I spent (almost) the whole, entire morning doing snowboarding practice.

We said **good morning** to the huskies on our way to the bunny slope. The three little pups were running around their mama, being cute and adorable again. ♥♥♥

I wonder what their names are?

And guess what we saw in the faraway distance?

A herd of beautiful brumbies, galloping through the trees! ♥♥♥

Cody and Layla were already practising when we finally arrived at the bunny slope. Cody is SOOO good. I'm going to try my absolute BEST to beat him tomorrow. Just as well I have my lucky dolphin snowboard to help me out. ☺

I was just doing a really excellent twisting turn when someone came WHIZZERING up behind me. SO FAST and SO CLOSE they almost knocked me off my board as they WHOOSHED past.

Someone wearing a crocodile ski jacket. ☹☹☹

And calling out my name. Like this.

~~Forch~~ Fortunately for me, I didn't lose my balance even a teeny tiny bit! And then Zoe and I WHOOSHED off down the hill together, like we'd been snowboarding our whole lives. ☺

But Flick started **wibbling and wobbling** away down the slope until . . .

He did a giganterous FLOP.

And guess who raced over to help him get back up again?

If you said Zoe and me you are 100 per cent to the power of 1000 WRONG! ☹☹☹

It was Cody! Zoe and I were so busy concentrating on getting our turns right we didn't even see him fall. Oops!

This is what we saw (and heard) when we finally stopped and looked back up the slope.

Looks like he didn't hurt himself TOO much though. (PHEWW.) But hopefully Flick will remember not to get quite so close to other people NEXT TIME he goes snowboarding. ☺

After that we kept on practising with Cody and Layla.

And guess what Zoe told me just now? She thinks I'm as good as Cody! SOOO good I could even win the big Crystal Mountain Beginners Snowboarding competition!

Zow-ie. I can't WAIT until tomorrow to find out. ☺

Have to stop now, Diary. Our families just arrived.

And they look REALLY cold. 😮

Ella

Friday afternoon, in my bunk (with a chair jammed under the door handle so no-one can come in)

Dear Diary,

I am in desperating despair. SOOO desperating I am not sure I will be able to write this next part.

But I will be VERY braverous and try.

After lunch Zoe and I went back outside into the windy wind so we could get our snowboards from the outdoor rack.

And mine was completely (and also utterly) gone. Even though I looked for it EVERYwhere.

Mum and Dad and the rest of our families came over to help me look.

But they couldn't find it either. It had completely disappeared. (And also ~~varnished~~ vanished.) ☹

And then I had a terrifyingly terrible (and also tragical) thought.

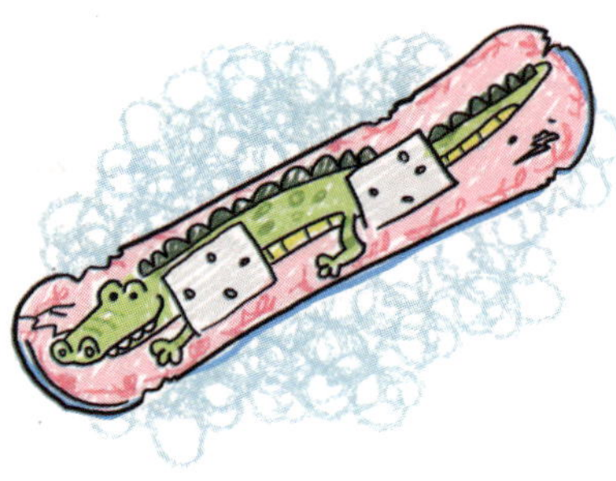

But guess what? They didn't. This is the ONLY board they had left.

No way ho-zay was I going to zoom down the slopes on an ~~anch~~ ancient old board with a snapperous crocodile on it. BLEUCHHH.

Also, people might think I was trying to look like Flick. DOUBLE BLEUCHHH!!!

I would rather spend the whole day (and night) playing noughts-and-crosses in the snow with Olivia.

It's SO not fair. ☹☹☹

Yours in desperation,
Ella
XOXO

About ten minutes later

I just had a horrendously horrible thought.

What if Flick accidentally on purpose took my dolphin snowboard?

And then hid it somewhere?

To stop me from going in the race!

😮😮😮

He wouldn't. Would he???

About another two minutes after that

Or . . .

WHAT IF THE YOWSER TOOK IT?!?!

😮😮😮😮😮😮

About five minutes after that

I still can't believe what happened next.

The door handle started rattling. And then there was a really louderous knock on the door.

KNOCK! KNOCK! KNOCK!

I was just about to call out: 'GO AWAY!' when a sweet little voice said, 'Ella! Let me in! I've just had the most BRILLIANT idea about your snowboard problem!'

Zoe ALWAYS has brilliant ideas about ways to solve problems. (Mostly.)

So I quickly wiped my eyes with the last tissue and climbed down from my top bunk so she could come in. Here's what we both said next.

Zoe (kindly): Don't worry, Ella. I have a plan.
Me (puzzled): You do?

Zoe (brightly): Yep. And it's excellent. You like horses, don't you?
Me (even more puzzled): Well, they're OK. I don't like them as much as dolphins though.
Zoe (brightlier): Then you can use my board in the big comp tomorrow. And I'll ask Mum to hire the crocodile one for me.
Me (gobsmacked): I didn't even know you liked crocodiles.
Zoe (smilingly): I do today. ☺
Me (tearily): Are you sure?
Zoe (smilinglier): Surer than sure. ☺

So we went back to the hire place with her mum, and she hired the crocodile (eww) board for Zoe.

And then Zoe gave her horsey one to me. Now we can both go in the race. Together!

Zoe is absolutely and totally the **besterest BFF EVER!**

Yours truly,

Ella

XOXO

Saturday morning, in bed, very, very early

Dear Diary.

I've just had the most WEIRDEREST dream in the history of weird dreams.

In my dream, I was lying on my bunk when I heard this whinnying and neighing and hoof-stampering sound. And outside my window were four beautiful brumbies. They were stamping their hooves in the snow to get my attention.

And standing on the back of the lead brumby was the lovely mama husky sled dog. And she was asking me if I'd seen her babies.

But then she (and also the brumbies) got chased away by a scary howling snow monster, with glowing googly eyes. And also a crocodile.

What does it all mean, Diary?

E x

Saturday, before lunch

Dearest Diary,

We had the skiing and snowboarding competitions!

I was **really nerverous** to the power of a pazillion about going in my section without my lucky snowboard. Even though Zoe had been kind (and also thoughtful) enough to give me hers.

But guess what? I didn't even need it! Who needs luck when you've got a BFF as good (and also fantabulous) as Zoe?

We whooshed down the bunny slope together, laughing and singing all the way. ☺

We didn't win. Cody did! But we didn't come last either. ☺

And guess what? As we were getting close to the finish line, who do you think fell over (again) trying to whoosh past Layla?

Flick! Only this time, Zoe and I DID STOP to help him up!

And then I had a thought. Maybe Flick's just not very good at balancing, like some of us are? Maybe he's not just a big pusherous meanie. Hmmm . . .

And if Zoe and I hadn't stopped to help him up we might have won the race! ☺

But who even cares? It was the MOST fun I have ever had in my whole, entire life! ☺

Uncle Lenny gave Zoe and I a trophy each for coming in equal fifth. And everyone clapped and cheered, really louderously!

Love,
Ella

About two hours later . . .

I found my lucky snowboard!

Well, ~~acksh~~ actually, someone else did. ☺

Carly and Lottie were having one last, final hike before they go home tomorrow.

And they were just trekking past some trees near the Crystal Cafe when they saw these!

So they brought them back up to the cafe to find their owners. And the cafe lady told them they'd all been blown away by the windy wind!

Which means Flick didn't take my snowboard after all. And neither did the Yowser!

(Though I'm still not completely 100 per cent sure it wasn't the Yowser . . .)

PHEW!

E

Saturday night, in bed

Dear Diary,

We've all just come back from the most aMAZing last night of a holiday ever!

There was a big festival in the village. With face-painting! And toasted marshmallows! And a real live band called **Chunky Monkey** that Zoe and I danced to with our new friends!

I even had a dance with Flick!

And then we all grabbed some **glowsticks** and climbed onto the chairlift with our families, for a final, last ride through the snowfields.

But the best thing that happened tonight was a giganterous fireworks display, from the very toppest part of the top of the mountain.

It was amazing. And excellent. And fanTABulously fabulous!

Good night
Sleep tight
Don't let
The crocodiles bite.
Or snap! ☺

Love,
Ella x

PS I'm not totally 100 per cent sure, but I think I saw someone (or something) running away into the dark while we were on the chairlift. Something with giganterous feet and glowing eyes . . .

Sunday, in the car

Dearest Diary,

We're on our way home again. (Sadly. ☹) Past the towering trees and the pretty birds and the sweet little bridge over the rushing river.

I even saw another echidna on the side of the road, waiting for our cars to go past. Maybe it was going back to its burrow to feed its baby. I wonder if it was the same one we saw before?

I can't wait to get home so I can write an Animal Fact File all about it. And also all the other amazing animals I saw while we were on Crystal Mountain.

Like the mountain pygmy possums. And the beautiful brumbies. And the howling huskies. And the . . .

The **YOWSER!**

After all, I saw its tracks.

And its glowing googly eyes. 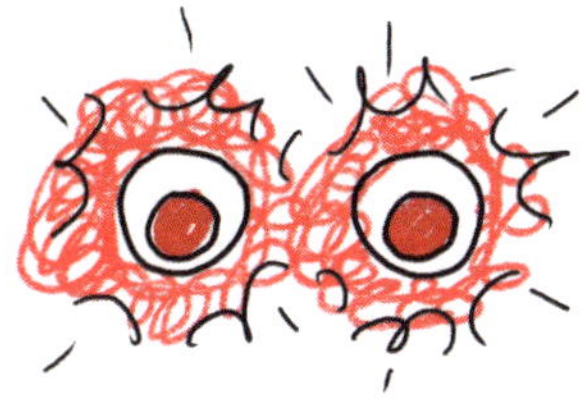

And I heard it HOWLING. Every. Single. Night.

So it MUST be real. Mustn't it?

Yours forever and ever,

Ella

XOXO

ELLA Diaries

Read more of Ella's brilliant diary!

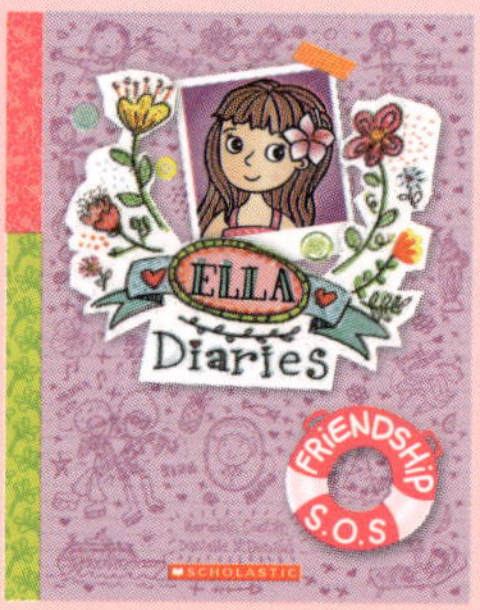

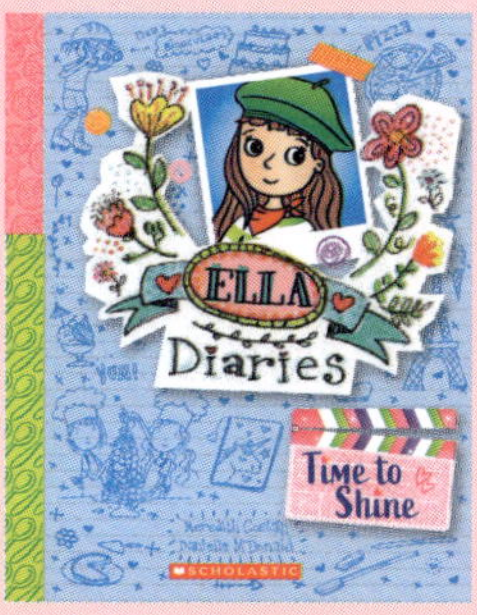

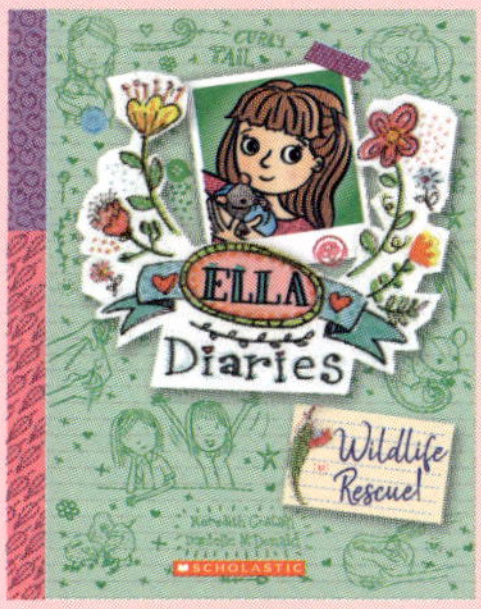

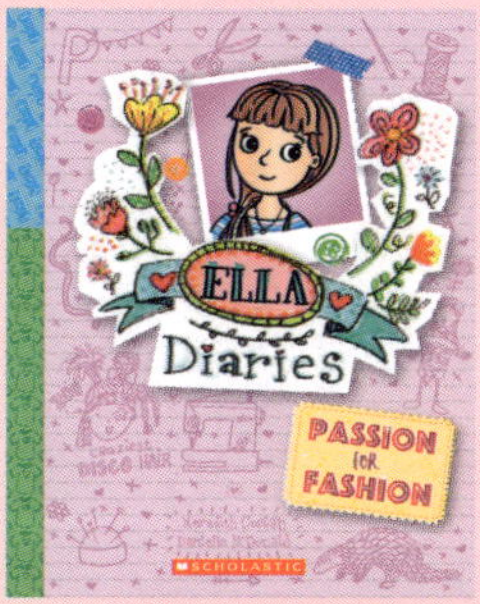

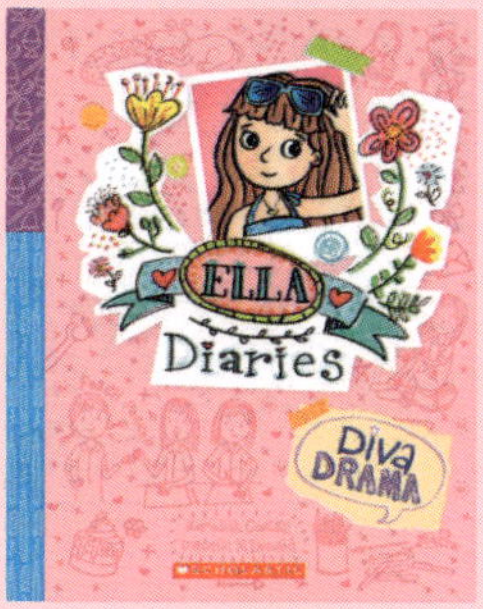

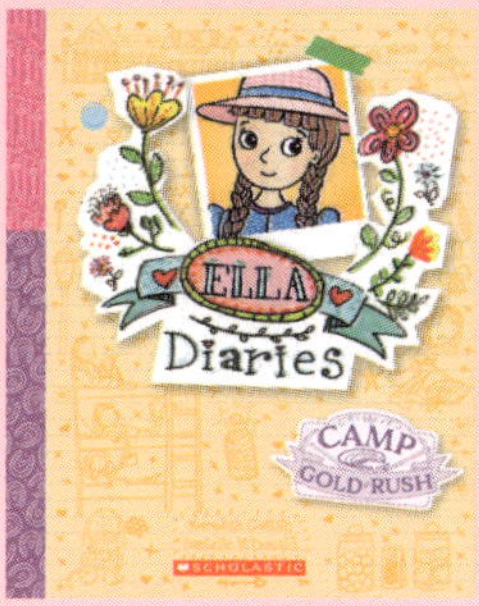

And look out for more coming soon!

FROM ELLA Diaries TO

ELLA AT EDEN

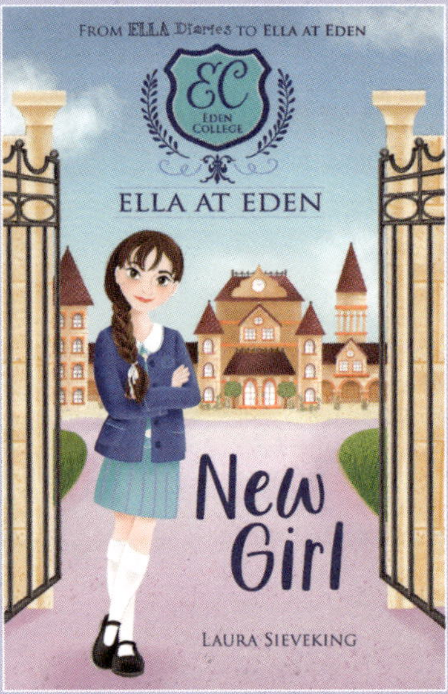

Ella has started at her new high school, and Eden College is everything she hoped it would be. She is getting to know her new friends and enjoying everything Eden has to offer. Until things start to get complicated. She accidentally insults Saskia, the school diva, there could be a ghost in the dorm, and items have started to mysteriously disappear. Can Ella catch the Eden thief?

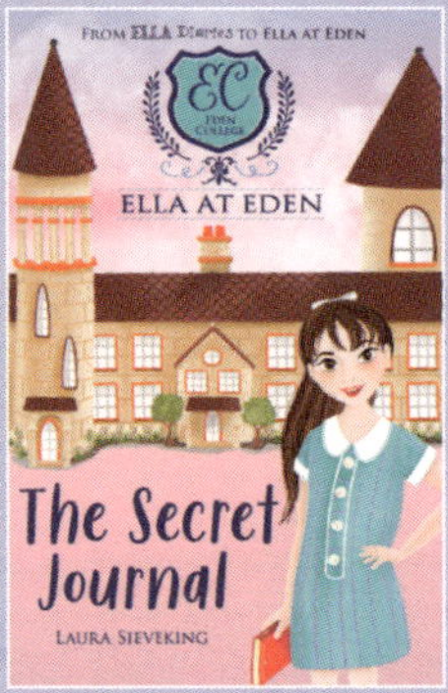

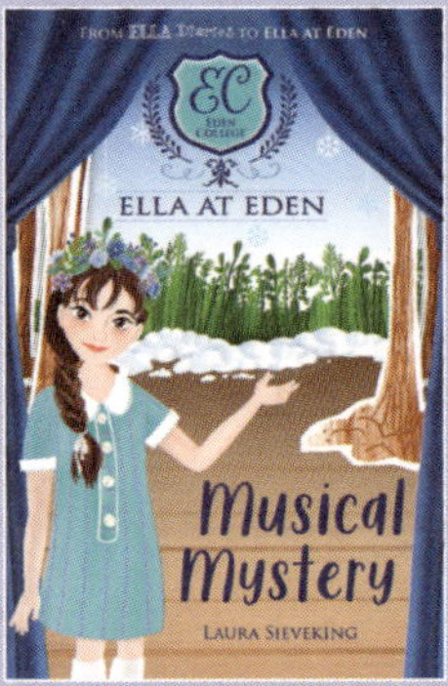